It Isn't a Ghost if It Lives in Your Chest

Also by Joan Houlihan

It Isn't a Ghost if It Lives in Your Chest

Joan Houlihan

Four Way Books
Tribeca

Library of Congress Cataloging-in-Publication Data

Names: Houlihan, Joan, 1951- author.
Title: It isn't a ghost if it lives in your chest / Joan Houlihan.
Other titles: It is not a ghost if it lives in your chest
Description: First edition. | New York : Four Way Books, [2021] |
Identifiers: LCCN 2021005299 | ISBN 9781945588914 (paperback)
Subjects: LCGFT: Poetry.
Classification: LCC PS3608.O85545 I85 2021 | DDC 811/.6--dc23
LC record available at https://lccn.loc.gov/2021005299

This book is manufactured in the United States of America and printed on
acid-free paper.

Four Way Books is a not-for-profit literary press. We are grateful for the assistance
we receive from individual donors, public arts agencies, and private foundations.

This publication is made possible with public funds from the
New York State Council on the Arts, a state agency.

We are a proud member of the Community of Literary Magazines and Presses.

Contents

/

//

///

You are this, which is so far from you.

—Jacques Lacan

The axe and hammer which come to be mother

Loud as the dark that comes over you,

to feed you, she forages here. Twigs break.

She is near the old parts of earth,

takes from its pressed-down matter

and makes an edible wafer.

When the churches died out, she stayed.

Her language busted with wrath.

Small mottles took hold of her skin.

Her body a warthog, she wobbled.

Truth in one hand, *Go to hell*, in the other,

she brandished the axe of *Justice*

as she floated over the stumps.

She brandished the hammer of *Dammit*

as we cowered in our beds.

Her will, made of pitch, can't be read.

Her Fostering

Mother is my thought.

She is leaf, then blue, then all

the blues together, high.

I am her eye.

She cooks me honey.

She cooks me milk.

She will always know me

by the pad of my feet in morning,

by the tip of my nose at noon,

by the tap-tap-tap of my cane at night.

The Cartwheel

The sun has gone in. The world is feeding.

Cooing dove, hooing owl—

in the cooling light I am strange to them.

Every night I am carried to bed

light as unbaled hay.

Every day at the root of the elm

my child-seat waits in weeds—

Chokewort. Blackmouth. Bristle-burr.

Cloud bales load to the sky.

Arms and legs, I am spokes on a lawn

fresh-cut. Which way am I turning, which way

am I facing? Ground. Sky. Ground.

A Species of Mother

Crooked seams and a garter belt,

daytime TV and a Whitman's sampler,

Queen for a Day with a twist—

she held us fixed in the sneer

of Widmark, his glee in pitching

a wheelchair down the stairs, Cagney

smashing half a grapefruit into a woman's face.

We kept quiet, nurtured ourselves on M&M's

and told each other the story of a forest

where mothers left children

in the care of a tender witch.

Occasionally, She Dreams

She tapped her chest. Her inside had gone.

Her synaptic gaps filled with night.

I don't know why I lie in bed.

I am always looking for my body and legs.

She no longer hears the sound of her voice.

If her mouth is closed, she can't find her teeth.

Occasionally, she dreams of a large gift of fruit:

Grapes look up to see her face.

Apples tell of their tree.

Pears hear her weep.

Plums proffer a pink solace.

Ward of the State

We housed her on the edge of a marsh

with calicos, tabbies, and a teacup pig.

They all ate together from a table by the window,

a horse leaning through.

Wild turkey spy. Geese push and bicker

on the lawn. A makeshift cross adorns it.

I don't belong in such a little house!

We told her it's just like her own.

She made collages.

There was no call for them.

Her travels were internal and through the eye.

Her memories came from inside a wall.

She wanted to get close, closer.

Of heaven I am the master key, she hummed,

hammering through plaster.

When we came with a writ and stamp,

she was thick with powder—a lady all over.

The Good Girl

Small humiliations: hair pulled, spanked

by her father, entered roughly by her husband,

mocked for her whimper. How did she stand it?

When she needed to kneel to the priest, when her mother

served crust dipped in milk: *poverty bread*.

Cardboard covered the holes in her shoes and she found

her peace in a rosary, mysteries on the large bead, murmurs

on the small. She was not there. She is not here.

I am holding her anyway for the first time at age 66

where she is: in a near-blue sky pinned with a gold star.

//

My Own Two Hands

Dented in infancy, head held

in a faulty manner, body

bundled in terry, I was

all natal all the time.

They who made me, made me

cocky and caustic, on everyone's nerves

and my own. Raised into a shout and fist,

feet taken from my walk,

torso turned toward the sun,

my two hands make silhouettes:

One, with a paddle raised, one cowering.

I call them *Truth* and *Reconciliation*.

I am a Switzerland

Father created an Alp for me.

He called it *Paaterhorn.*

It came out in the shape of a sugar cone,

the top, silvery-white.

Am I an heiress? Yes!

To his hymn book with gilt edge.

To his Bible's pressed-to-death pansies and moth.

To these brass cufflinks and trouser hangers.

To this sprung Eros in my damask.

What pink flesh you have, he'd observe,

as he stuffed an apple into a pig head

and served it with both eyes open.

He worked his own eyes from behind,

a large contraption moving room to room,

made like an icon: by looking.

Born into his country, I master him.

My eyes, hands, and ears triumph.

In winter, my Alp is powdered with Father,

his head a silvery cloud.

Birth Order

My first child came out

sewn together from rags.

We fostered a makeshift dependence—

me, a child myself from birth

who had nothing to reckon by,

she, a notion, covered in cloth

made by will and want.

By night she unwraps

down to nothing and lies at my feet.

By day she pulls herself together and speaks:

Mother, you shall be loved by me

and covered with abundance.

We sit at the window together, content:

two branches on sky, two deer by a fence.

I am a Fugitive from a Chain Gang

Blinded by freedom and without morals,

unable to follow orders, family

a partially digested memory,

I have left the problem known as people.

The past comes on as illness—

how we twisted together, clanked ankles

and smelled like heat. Depraved, rubbing

sand in the palms of our hands, from above

our line writhed like de Havilland's snake pit.

Now I have become my own prisoner,

drinking from a bowl of river water,

playing with the head of an axe.

Where does kindness come from? Not here.

The Voyage

Candle lit in the hold, insecure on the boards,

I've forgotten why I undertook this voyage.

As the ship rocks, shadows flow over

embedded mosses, pockmarks riddle

the walls, waver into faces. No!

I don't want to be here. The weather is water

and doesn't belong to me, the candle

smudges smoke to corners.

I miss the feel of land, the leaf-lit streets

of autumn, the hill that loved my bicycle,

let down its spine so long, so lovely, so kind;

the wind, the trailing sun, the small work

of building snow-cities in hedges, their roofs

powder under my swept mitten—

Could I return? To hedge-light, paw print,

ant and leaf, to the shook leaves on my street,

to the long-loving injury I called life?

I am simpler here at sea, but I might not be well.

This matter can't be handled calmly in a pharmacy,

blue-lit, red and trembling *welcome* on its door,

or by a doctor, ether rising from his coat,

the plangent striking of a drill or blade, the dosing

and pungency of alchemic liquids,

the way he sticks the hypodermic deep into my mouth

like a prayer. With all these bottles glowing, none of them,

opened, release me. This is the riddle of the bottle—

the wish evaporates once the cotton is removed.

What knocks against the hull moves loud

to soft, creaks and bangs as if a body

is thrown against a door. Who's there?

The candle gutters. I trust a sudden flare

to light me in the hold, for someone to see

the child down here, to carry me up from the dark.

The Twins

Where's Ansel? The hairs rise up.

Arthur remembers him. All that's left is a skin.

He recalls their walk in the woods, two brindle-colored

pit bulls who threw out barks like laughs

and the black bear who stood on his hind legs and snorted,

then wobbled away, looking back.

One thing I remember about Ansel is this—

Arthur crosses his arms at his face,

curves into a stoop, kneels to the ground

and begs. Then he laughs—*It wasn't a black bear!*

It was a brown boar! It came out of the woods,

grinned at us. Then ran. Arthur remembers

how the two dogs loved each other

from the corners of their eyes, how the trouble began

in their bond. How Ansel's pieces were ripped and strewn.

Education

Out and alone, I wander

and wonder: where do shadows go?

Father's, gigantic, blocks the sun.

He moves to let it blind me.

Know thyself. Know thyself.

I have been paralyzed by this.

I once spoke thus and such,

taught the young to examine their lives.

I told them their gods were dirty.

Now I am smaller and make figures on the wall—

cow nodding, floppy turkey, birdy-on-a-branch.

Little Plato is my rabbit.

He nibbles on my scrolls.

Corpus Glorification

In hospice, by moonlight,

part of him crawls nocturnal, cold,

through the smell of resin,

the pine-gods solemn and tall.

Part of him speaks to himself:

Lay yourself down in the ground, Sir.

Then comes floating a funeral,

which never touches the ground.

He stands to watch it go by.

The evening is a room.

Prepared and empty, he goes in.

From the clock he can hear a little death-talk.

Ghosts in profile, middle-aged and older,

their bottom halves trailing off,

walk into and out of the room,

lonely and stray. He asks:

How can I be standing here, if I am in the ground?

And the wall, and the nurse, and the clock,

all look, and the moon waves from every window

as they wrap him up from top to toe in a very fine veil.

Hagiography

I belong to a room on the slope of an Alp

in a house for people down-at-the-heels.

Mother mends linen for the highers-up,

the ones in chalets with curly eaves,

balconies whipped into peaks.

They look down on us

through windows latticed like pies.

At three, I saw the shade of living light.

At eight, I was enclosed as an oblate.

The universe is an egg, I said,

and the nuns promoted me.

When I refused to tell what I heard from God,

I was sent an illness that paralyzed my limbs.

My ceiling is pierced with holes.

They used a trephine.

Searchlights pour through all night.

Who are they looking for?

My trundle bed wheels to the top of the stairs.

Without seeing anyone, I drink the last

from a cup, keep Mother's needle inside my sleeve.

I never hurt anyone. This is why they sainted me.

Ghostlier Demarcations

O Sean Fitzgerald, tell me, if you know,

why my grave is staggered here

on this small hill in Concord,

among the hundred and a hundred

crowded in, their markers thin,

the alders in their afternoon glory.

O Sean, you sly old bone,

tell me why a Pentecostal sun

stains the leaves to glass and shines

through branches arched, ornate and deep,

to form a nave above me where I sleep.

O shadow-man! O tick-tock!

Tell me, if you care to, why among the trunks

the elders soft in step and coughing, tread.

I must call my brother straightaway. O, but he is dead.

Too much to drink. Like you.

Why can't you people cast the habit off?

O Sean Fitzgerald, hark, you drunk, and tell me

why the trees release their undemanding leaves

to earth, and at the root, a footed mushroom, blue,

thrives in their decay—

I don't believe you can.

You think because I speak to you I am alone. No.

Mother-doll abides here too,

and father-doll has gone to sleep after his drink.

Their daughter, I—a carve of angel-stone

bowed over me—lie here too.

O Fitz, the trees have shed.

I hear your steps, your rake,

as lightly through the leaves it goes,

the crackle you make over me.

Tell me if you know—when will I be free?

The Gift Horse

I saw her at the side of the lane—

the face of a saint, fierce and Byzantine.

That's how she looked

when she knew she would die.

Once you know you will die, the sky flattens.

Stars poke their fingers through

and point at you.

She was holding the little cloth horse

I gave her. I pried it loose.

That summer there was a surge in mice.

The noise of their feet in my yard—!

I no longer enjoy a cup of tea

or a simple walk in the lane.

Thank you for coming here.

My head feels like someone's hammering.

It's high time I was cared for.

Once upon a rehab

A hero of the highest order, I came here freely

and was shorn of my self-regard like a merino sheep

of its wool. I can no longer sleep.

My left arm can't forget how hard it tried on the crutch.

I lie down and it aches its hatred of me.

I know the electricity in a bulb is different

from the electricity they run across your scalp—

one is not restrained. That's the one they run on me

at night. It gives me unwelcome reception to people

I don't know. They say I will walk one day.

They are building my blood back up

from the bags they took from me.

They jiggle my meat with paddles,

play wheel-go-round with my legs.

It takes an alteration of will. What I will.

Look out the window, they say.

I can't enjoy what I see. I will never leave here.

I was the kid with the drum

The rivets we pounded went in solid,

and we built a tower of brick and lime,

sat on the beams and ate our lunches

legs swinging over the city.

Torches high we walked the rails

hammered in spikes, made the steel sing

and it sang on the tracks that take us now

to side-yards and small, pointed fires.

No sky before us, no sky behind,

we ride knees up in the boxcar-dark.

Stained with sweat from the tracks,

stained with earth from the fields,

the marvelous harvest staunched,

why should I now be standing in line,

hands in the shape of a bowl?

Every day goes and I want to go too

with that huge, still harvest of men.

Tabernacle Time

Sin displayed a stain, a drop of ink

in a bowl of milk. A cross came.

A man with a hammer and nails came.

Novenas came, glass beads

skimming fingers came, and the chip

off an old saint's bone shone under cellophane.

While the gold plate quivered under my chin,

I felt the priest place a wafer on my tongue.

Body of Christ, he winked.

My Left Hand

I want to stop thinking

about where it goes, about

when it will come back.

I don't need you, I hiss to the dark.

My right hand finds it, touches it.

They have a language, a birthplace, together.

In the morning, I'm shown the mirror.

I see it reflected and cry with relief.

It comes to my face to wipe the tears.

///

Blind trust,

in the nod of a cow, stiff-legged,

as she leaps in the paddock, drops

to her knees, then back, to roll on new grass—

The large eye caresses yours. She smells you

as you lead her through the shaded field.

Hooded and without guile, follows you

to the chute. You are the ignorance

she lives through, the heavy blade she hears

sliding into the grooves.

The secret brutalities will make patties from that

on your behalf. A human fraternity

carved out of a hung carcass.

Charles at Down House

Out of every crevice, plants feel,

twist and corkscrew toward light.

The tip of the radicle tickles its embryo

as all tendrils come close,

bee-laden, over the bean.

Everything goes on—

Forest floors paved with a breccia of bone.

Trunks with scars of different ages.

The height of cliffs, the age of seas,

the dusky ink of an octopus turning

hyacinth-red to ebon, hiding

the hole from which it crawled.

Now, velvet slippers and tea.

I listen with my cupboard mouse

to the loud, strange cry of black,

stained in its own survival.

The Damaged Parrot

Slow as a child first out,

she moved through worlds of trees and grass,

fell asleep in the sun while the other birds played,

woke in the dark and expelled her owner's words:

Oh snap! Crap! Baby want a bitch-slap?

Felt herself to be green but never knew her head was red,

worked on finding food at night so no one could see—

peeling bark off trees, pecking at leaves.

Got the hang of seeds. Went with the gang

to neighborhood feeders, finally fitting in.

Tomorrow, she will come again and, dawdling, stand

large among the chickadees, finally free of speech.

Our Good Animals

The head of one, punched through the wall,

looks down at us, completes the room.

Curly horns offset his deadpan stare.

The long-snouted gator, shunned for his teeth

once ran on little bent legs: humble and low

to the ground. He was droll and fast.

We are faster, of course. And tall.

His skin belts our pants, gives us gloves.

I own a horse-hair handbag!

I, an ivory ring!

I, a jar with two bear claws holding it!

I, a zebra rug!

I've heard the necks of giraffes hum,

seen them startle and fold as they run,

seen elephants circle a baggy calf,

still-birthed, on its side. They trumpet

and stamp dust up. Unseemly, their trunks

hang down. Their heads are much bigger than ours.

Yet we are so much smarter.

My tabby expands her patterns in sun, to match

my oriental rug. Her noise is gone. She's been

declawed. But the fur!

You can't buy it in artificial form.

You need it alive and able to feel—

beauty moving under your hand.

Eco-friendly

High leaves waft over roots' deep

drink, as under one leaf and another we'll come

to know how far, how small, how between

splendor and animal crawl we are.

People will remember us won't they?

Of course they will. Until they don't.

The body has bones as a stay, doesn't it?

Yes, but who wants to? I have no wish to see

turtles unshell, trees in a palsy,

dehydrated snakes on dust. The rabbit damage alone

will be ghastly. Let's away to higher land.

We'll spy our last bird, a parrot gone silent,

the final caterpillar bunched on a stick.

Let's prize these hours when we believed we'd live.

Trigger Warning

On what were said to be tarpaulins,

by campsite, our fish pan empty,

god-awful stings on our fronts and backs,

appendages ending in fingers, all that—

it brings forth the time of my shock.

We rummaged our rucksacks for crumbs

in the cracks of our leather linings.

Some of us lifted our guns—

Nature. It's here for us.

The squirrel bit, the bird bit,

and bear. Loaded for you

they rise big from a bush,

typically drag you around

then stuff you under a log—

a meal to come back to, enjoy.

Nine-tenths of the law and all that.

I waited for hours playing dead,

then used my fingers to dig my way out.

The dirt's still under my nails.

My Bird, Myself

Dwarf plants, brittle green,

a premature llama, a white giraffe

splashed clean, a pouter pigeon

with an inflatable crop.

These are the limit of my estate.

The first pouter came out as a double-tail,

made from the ancient rock pigeon.

An experiment that changed its cry

five times. It was a private study.

Privacy causes asylums, doesn't it?

My doctor's listening, performed

with a stethoscope, pins me to meaning

I didn't mean. An academic,

reeking of the study.

I don't deserve him.

He speaks and I no longer listen.

My pouter rests on a spliced tree,

scars of different ages

giving it all the history it needs.

Topologically Yours

This ground is heaving graves.

What's underfoot has business here,

but the whole landscape looks like trash.

A body speaks to you from behind:

I'm a bitter kind of happy.

Bodies have feelings too.

In its own head it tried to be kind—

Now it misses being killed.

Soon you won't have any land

so storm over this one with long strides.

Go higher. Echoes around the hills

never stop. Take a lesson from that—

No one can hear you.

I hemorrhaged like a rose. Fold after fold.

Here comes another sunset.

Don't lose your eyes to it.

The children have gone

Housed in your drawer, their sharps and caps,

pistols and the jackknife tucked back.

Their fetal cells embedded in you, a sting in your throat

as they wept. Your body, a cotton, assuaged them.

Now molded with evening's purple, the cotton

is cloud the wind bales, builds and makes noble in bulk.

From bud to full-blown, the children have gone.

Snow on the grass has become a crust

lifted up on the heads of blades, and many hares sit

on open hills, still, and in purple shadow.

Lined with defeat

Snow cover | spoiled

by Fennec | fox-rust

pricked ears | and paw-

print | breath | crystallized

in lungs | and blood | spot-lit on snow—

I will track her. | She will tire, lie down.

Curling cold | shades wrap

her bed | closed.

I stab the fire in her | the blood in her.

Brava! | Little death | go into my mouth.

This world hunts.

My war grows frail

because it goes on and on, bones

bothered with age, hands

troubled with shakes, face

mottled with spots.

Because its hearing has been lost

and people keep talking, yelling,

Look out! when the bombs blow.

Because it's been shot, stunned, burnt,

and comes back weakened, but comes back.

Because it can't run away and sort of hops.

Because it mistakes harm for kindness

and smiles at the one who stops, smiles

as he raises his arm to take a closer shot.

Because it's slow and deposits itself like snow

all over the battlefield. Because it doesn't mind

lying down and staying there. Because snow is beautiful.

The Enemy

We don't look at them, they look at us—

our lowered pig heads, grunt in our snouts,

a last burst of flame in our thighs,

our cries for mother as the knife loves us—

then one by one, piece by pound,

they gather us, squealing, to their ground.

My Noah

His doctrine on heads, renowned.

His research on pain, advanced.

A yearning for purity drives his surgeries.

Doctor, I am at sea,

alone since my husband died.

I listened to years of sawing,

years of "almost there."

After his care, I'll reach land.

On my prow, the dove;

from my brow, every animal paired.

////

The Wedding

Mother stood in the parlor—

an upright no one could play.

Father handed his business around.

We hired a minister laced with mirth

who couldn't pronounce the word *lilac.*

In days to come, we hung ancient maps,

stashed lumber in the pantry.

Everyone knows what marriage is,

but we knew nothing.

They told us not to cry with our mouths.

We could cry with our eyes if we had to.

The rooms we moved through

were quiet and tall, wrought with ivy.

My Late Idiot

Has gone far from the bed-sit he sat in

with a view of the business end of a mouse.

Saves soap-shavings for the years to come.

Eats from a bowl that doubles as a cup.

Steers his old horse, a silver walker.

Now that he's gone I have no one

who's not all there, no one

with an IQ of moderate to severe.

Day secretes time. Air rattles my door.

At night he surrounds the planet.

Bottle Dungeon

We stood inside looking up.

The brow of the *Pont des Arts,*

its nasty heart-shaped padlocks

cast from brass, filled with cuts

and tetanus, rose over the Seine.

Tourists stood another view: a tree that curled

its bark, a promenade of small pillow-

dogs, walkers with lion-headed walking sticks

who waved silk scarves while they talked—

Shall I reach over the rail for a fig, dear?

Or will it prove sour?

What a beautiful silence we made.

Like the tower clock's stopped hands

from which a man once hung.

We set his place as before

The chair with arms, for status.

The wedding china, white and gold.

Geranium in the middle, bowed.

Billie's voice on the phonograph, cracked.

We hung his suit in the shape of him,

placed his suitcase beside it.

Where am I going again?

Outside, his tools lay rusted, re-inventions

of himself, a hazardous waste

between mice and sky

we had to pay to get rid of.

The Talk

It wasn't about your face, or

that you shut yourself away, or

about your teeth and money.

We kept to our shrunken isle

dry of spirit, empty of music,

a poached interior, around us the water.

The years receded.

Off in the head and mutual, the suffering

of trying to know as the talk

lowered to our fingertips, touched.

When you died, I took you with me.

Breathes from the body uncanny

A cloth on the mouth,

a box for a head,

a bright liquid hole in the eye—

We are nothing if not our body

in thrall to a younger day.

C'mon out, it's a curds-and-whey sky!

Mottles and combs and sprays!

And bunny, swift to the woods,

and bunny, into the bush!

Now my face is gone long,

yours is gone bye.

Apples sink to the field.

Lilacs limp out and bow.

Oh, for our days strung childlike,

our evenings stung hard with stars!

Host

Let's reach into you.

What have we here?

From convalescence to blood on a plate—

let's be blunt: soaked, pinched

and measured, now you're a man who can't feel.

The technology of ministration is icy and obscure.

Animals are better. Weaned of light, a horse

would rather soften in its stall

than die in the open and shame us.

It took us ten minutes to take off your shirt

and what do we see? A white patch

where you wore a watch.

Let's button you up,

make you ready for your guests.

Spousal

Our faults crept like fungus over bark.

The difference? Shades of decay.

Mine being lighter.

We were in our own hospital then.

You didn't know me,

only my scent and lack of courtesy.

You acted original, boastful of your designer robe,

invented a non-spill bedpan and needle-free IV line.

Something to look forward to.

See my wig?

Woven over time, like my attachment to you.

Rather than suffer through, let's work on a burial.

I'll probably end up on the mantel with you.

But I want to be by the sea.

Account of a Root

Rising improbable in pajamas,

out at the elbows, ripped at the knees,

mum to the bone, mouth-ready—

He still hasn't found a face.

I called him a bum and I'm sorry.

You look like a horse after mucking, I'd said,

you look like a bleeding mouse.

What shit! he cried from his top,

hitched up his bottom and huffed.

His symptom? Tympanic. The drum, the drum.

Then a shout from the bedroom:

I'm under! I'm under!

I pulled him out like a root.

Our Story

I treat animal memory

as the foundation of identity

and you, precious gelding,

coat stroked to transparency,

I see through your rampage,

your lively horse laugh.

How long can I lead you

with such a worn halter?

Once, on a road that slants down just a little,

in the confidence of a morning

we started out.

The Carving

I have a habit of sleeping in my clothes

away from the loud and mute, kill time

by carving your figure from soap, dipping it

in melted pitch. I set it alight. Set it afloat.

When the soap fails to come back,

I search as a boat, far out.

Your bed, a burning deck, lights the way.

Soaked Through and Vanishing

To secure the halo of home—

a deceit painted on thick—

how else could our silence

hold him, his grandiose talk

and two missing teeth?

Anonymous, intimate, homely as hell,

he sat in his chair, prepared.

Afterwards, we chucked it to the yard,

stains everywhere.

Tell-tale

X-rays show where the parts are,

what pieces come from

where. The rogue organs,

the way they built another body

inside yours—a home away from home—

gave us somewhere to live while we waited.

Made from time, the disquiet

reached into the world, touched

your shirt, your pants,

that bone-sheath you called your skin,

this cup you put your mouth to,

that I now put to mine.

Custom

You on your last day bled

a sunset spread on a rag.

I touch the past like a chair.

From custom, I burn a candle.

I have not found your face.

Late of Sargent Street

Ivory lamps held high, your magnolia tree

lights the porch—wood-laid, oiled and fussed over—

and across my eye, a grackle, hooded in shine, struts

the garden's crumble where the red and lavish smoke-

bush bends, defrocked, all sticks. Now leaves stacked or blown

to stiff and crackling waves, circle

the porch rails, fill the door jamb, prevent its opening

to where a last copper flash—perhaps

of bowl or clock or hair—returns me

to the year-long dread, the tremor

of your hand moving across the sheet.

Care

Come to your robe.

Come to the table.

Your egg cup is empty.

You can't find your egg.

It cries so you don't have to.

Soft, into a toast.

The Angel

About your talking: it's worse.

Your bed has not been slept in.

A hand pulls the drape,

guides you by the elbow

without permission, away.

She knows you

by your scent, the shape

of your hair. Likes to look

in your wardrobe, count what's there.

Walks you down the stairs.

You are covered in veins

and your velvet robe hangs

from your shoulders, looser. It sways.

Winged and sly, she bends to you.

You are holy prey.

Law

Upheld by writ, by star or

spine seen through a fish—

you learn in bed, pressed under

the weight of legal tender, hear

in the eaves stuffed with nest,

a rustle, a loaded reckoning.

The Girl I Left Behind Me

The wind, being motherless, wraps the tree,

troubles the window a little.

My kittens circle, crouch, leap

couch to counter and back,

and in the detritus of me,

box to box to tiniest box, I

unpack the single pussy willow—

one paw tissued—

in that velvet-dark I moved through

lit low in spite of others, heat

enough for me, enough

for others to refrain from.

I rub the amber leaf light

from my last Christmas tree,

take to the tub and marble surround

to worship the waters, take

to the bed heaped high and deep,

my appetite caged and cruelly tamed.

Who will make me safe, conspire in the lie

of beauty, the lie of the body

unbreached? In the rush of tissue, new

boots laced to my pace, cincture of suede

at my waist, and my hair—
my god, the waves of shook

copper shining a girl's will—
How far I've come!

And how do you like your hyacinth girl,
the gone-as-smoke of me, now.

The Harbinger

I like paralysis best—

someone I can carry uphill, in a blizzard,

staggering across a parking lot, or

lifting them, hot, from bed to chair.

I am broad-backed and without PTSD.

My damage protects me

from you. I am a human fire, burning

with know-how you will never know.

I can give care because I don't care.

Made of padding and string hair,

a plaster chest-plate pierced with spikes

I can remove, I'm not in need.

Several homes ago I stopped being seen

and can now see through you.

I cross your threshold—cross yourself.

Everyone is leaving. I am the only one left.

Sunset, Fir Tree, Star

Sunset flows north.

A river flows under its shell.

I left the house to get lost.

To make the tree visible.

I put out limbs to illuminate

the inside of my body.

Why should I care what goes away?

The star, which is out of this world, flourishes.

There is a meadow, afterward

Soft hammers of the brain provide

the number of times you've died.

Your voice pitched to where I can't hear it.

This is my drift—

brief iris, mown grass, dates on a stone.

I am happy where I am, where we are—

not a sky on it, not a ground,

stepping between years, a mourner

making slow work of it.

Tucked Underground

They close history down.

They drink the milk of dark.

In our glassware and balsam,

in an orange pierced with clove,

in a tree and its pointed star,

we are here, in the rooms above.

Notes

In "A Species of Mother," the reference to "Widmark" is to the actor Richard Widmark in "Kiss of Death (1947); and "Cagney" is to the actor James Cagney in "The Public Enemy" (1931). "Queen for a Day" was a popular game show in the late '40s and '50s wherein housewives with the best sob stories won big prizes, usually appliances. A "garter belt" was used by women in the '50s to hold up nylon stockings.

"I am a Fugitive from a Chain Gang" is the name of a 1932 movie in which a World War I veteran (Paul Muni) is wrongly convicted of a robbery and sentenced to prison and a brutal chain gang, from which he escapes. "de Havilland's snake pit" refers to the actress Olivia de Havilland, who plays a woman confined to a mental institution and the term for the worst level in the institution. The term was originally used to describe a treatment of the mentally ill consisting of throwing the ill person into a pit of snakes with the intent of scaring them back into sanity. That movie, made in 1948, is called "The Snake Pit."

"I was the kid with the drum" is a line from the popular Great Depression song "Brother, Can You Spare a Dime?"

"Ghostlier Demarcations" is from the last line of "Idea of Order at Key West" by Wallace Stevens.

"The Girl I left Behind Me" is the title of the painting by Eastman Johnson, circa 1872, that Lucie Brock-Broido intended as the cover for her next book, now unfinished.

"There is a meadow, afterward" is a line from Lucie Brock-Broido's poem, "A Meadow," and is the epitaph on her gravestone in Mt. Auburn Cemetery, Cambridge, Massachusetts.

Acknowledgments

Thanks to the editors of the following publications where some of these poems first appeared:
The Banyan Review, IMAGE, Ocean State Review, On the Seawall, Passenger, Plume, Salamander

The Eloquent Poem, edited by Elise Paschen (Persea Press)
Plume Poetry 8, edited by Daniel Lawless

Joan Houlihan's five previous books of poetry include, most recently, *Shadow-feast* (Four Way Books, 2018), named a must-read by the Massachusetts Center for the Book. Her other collections are: *Hand-Held Executions* (Del Sol Press, 2003 & reprinted 2009); *The Mending Worm* (New Issues Press, 2006 & reprinted 2021), winner of the Green Rose Award; *The Us* (Tupelo Press, 2009), named a must-read by the Massachusetts Center for the Book; and the sequel *Ay* (Tupelo Press, 2014).

In addition to publishing in a wide array of journals, including *Boston Review, Columbia: A Journal of Literature and Arts, Gettysburg Review, Gulf Coast, Harvard Review, Poetry, Poetry International*, and *Taos Journal of International Poetry and Art*, her poems have been anthologized in *Iowa Anthology of New American Poetries,* Reginald Shepherd, ed. (University of Iowa Press, 2005); *The Book of Irish-American Poetry, 18th Century to Present*, Daniel Tobin, ed. (University of Notre Dame, 2007); *The World Is Charged: Poetic Engagements with Gerard Manley Hopkins*, William Wright and Daniel Westover, eds. (Clemson University Press, 2016); and *The Eloquent Poem,* Elise Paschen, ed. (Persea Press, 2020).

She currently serves on the faculty of Lesley University's Low-Residency MFA in Creative Writing Program in Cambridge, Massachusetts and is Professor of Practice in Poetry at Clark University in Worcester, Massachusetts. Houlihan founded and directs the Colrain Poetry Manuscript Conference.

Publication of this book was made possible by grants and donations. We are also grateful to those individuals who participated in our 2020 Build a Book Program. They are:

Anonymous (14), Robert Abrams, Nancy Allen, Maggie Anderson, Sally Ball, Matt Bell, Laurel Blossom, Adam Bohannon, Lee Briccetti, Therese Broderick, Jane Martha Brox, Christopher Bursk, Liam Callanan, Anthony Cappo, Carla & Steven Carlson, Paul & Brandy Carlson, Renee Carlson, Cyrus Cassells, Robin Rosen Chang, Jaye Chen, Edward W. Clark, Andrea Cohen, Ellen Cosgrove, Peter Coyote, Janet S. Crossen, Kim & David Daniels, Brian Komei Dempster, Matthew DeNichilo, Carl Dennis, Patrick Donnelly, Charles Douthat, Morgan Driscoll, Lynn Emanuel, Monica Ferrell, Elliot Figman, Laura Fjeld, Michael Foran, Jennifer Franklin, Sarah Freligh, Helen Fremont & Donna Thagard, Reginald Gibbons, Jean & Jay Glassman, Ginny Gordon, Lauri Grossman, Naomi Guttman & Jonathan Mead, Mark Halliday, Beth Harrison, Jeffrey Harrison, Page Hill Starzinger, Deming Holleran, Joan Houlihan, Thomas & Autumn Howard, Elizabeth Jackson, Christopher Johanson, Voki Kalfayan, Maeve Kinkead, David Lee, Jen Levitt, Howard Levy, Owen Lewis, Jennifer Litt, Sara London & Dean Albarelli, David Long, James Longenbach, Excelsior Love, Ralph & Mary Ann Lowen, Jacquelyn Malone, Donna Masini, Catherine McArthur, Nathan McClain, Richard McCormick, Victoria McCoy, Ellen McCulloch-Lovell, Judith McGrath, Debbie & Steve Modzelewski, Rajiv Mohabir, James T. F. Moore, Beth Morris, John Murillo & Nicole Sealey, Michael & Nancy Murphy, Maria Nazos, Kimberly Nunes, Bill O'Brien, Susan Okie & Walter Weiss, Rebecca Okrent, Sam Perkins, Megan Pinto, Kyle Potvin, Glen Pourciau, Kevin Prufer, Barbara Ras, Victoria Redel, Martha Rhodes, Paula Rhodes, Paula Ristuccia, George & Nancy Rosenfeld, M. L. Samios, Peter & Jill Schireson, Rob Schlegel, Roni & Richard Schotter, Jane Scovell, Andrew Seligsohn & Martina Anderson, James & Nancy Shalek, Soraya Shalforoosh, Peggy Shinner, Dara-Lyn Shrager, Joan Silber, Emily Sinclair, James Snyder & Krista Fragos, Alice St. Claire-Long, Megan Staffel, Bonnie Stetson, Yerra Sugarman, Dorothy Tapper Goldman, Marjorie & Lew Tesser, Earl Teteak, Parker & Phyllis Towle, Pauline Uchmanowicz, Rosalynde Vas Dias, Connie Voisine, Valerie Wallace, Doris Warriner, Ellen Doré Watson, Martha Webster & Robert Fuentes, Calvin Wei, Bill Wenthe, Allison Benis White, Michelle Whittaker, and Ira Zapin.